A CHILD'S FIRST BIBLE STORYBOOK

A CHILD'S FIRST BIBLE STORYBOOK

Sandol Stoddard

PICTURES BY
Tony Chen

An Inspirational Press Book for Children

CONSULTANTS

Father John Paul Engelcke
Vicar of the Church of the Holy Cross, Oahu, Hawaii: editor of the *Hawaiian Church Chronicle*; former Episcopal chaplain, University of Hawaii

Mary Ann Getty, RSM, Ph.D
Doctorate from University of Louvain, Belgium; Associate Editor of *The Bible Today*, *Catholic Biblical Quarterly*, and *Catholic Study Bible* (Oxford University Press), formerly of Catholic University and Carlow College.

Baruch A. Levine
Professor of Hebrew and Judaic Studies, New York University; author of JPS Torah Commentary in *Leviticus*; former Guggenheim Fellow.

Book design by November and Lawrence, Inc.
Art direction by Diana Klemin

First Inspirational Press edition published in 1998.

Inspirational Press
A division of BBS Publishing Corporation
386 Park Avenue South
New York, NY 10016

Inspirational Press is a registered trademark of BBS Publishing Corporation.

Published by arrangement with GuildAmerica® Books,
an imprint and trademark of Doubleday Direct, Inc., Dept. GB, 401 Franklin Avenue, Garden City, New York 11530.

Library of Congress Catalog Card Number: 98-72396

ISBN: 0-88486-215-1

Printed in Mexico.

To my family—

especially P.R.G.

A Child's First Bible Storybook was written with respect for the Protestant, Catholic, and Jewish biblical and religious traditions. My main texts have been in the *Jerusalem*, the *New Oxford*, the *Revised Standard*, and the *King James* Bibles. Some inevitable choices had to be made—for example, various traditions divide and number the Ten Commandments differently; and intertestamental material, such as the story of the Maccabees, is not always included. I am very grateful to the artist, Tony Chen, to my editors and art director, and in particular, for the advice and encouragement I have received, to Father John Paul Engelcke, Dr. Mary Ann Getty, and Professor Baruch A. Levine. Each has helped me toward my goal, which has been not to retell stories from the Bible yet again, but rather to reflect quite directly as much of the Bible's own compelling truth and beauty as possible in a very limited space, and in the plainest of language.

Contents

THE
·OLD TESTAMENT·

HOW GOD MADE THE WORLD

IN THE BEGINNING there was nothing at all but the Spirit of God moving like wind over dark waters. Then God said, "Let there be light!" and there was light. God saw that the light was good, and called it *day.* And the darkness God called *night.* This was the first day.

On the second day, God made the sky and called it *heaven.*

On the third day, God sent the water from the land and called the dry land *earth.* "Let there be growing things on earth," said God. And so there were plants and trees and flowers. And God saw that they were good.

On the fourth day, God made the sun and the moon and the stars.

On the fifth day, God said, "Let there be fishes in the sea, and birds in the air." And so there were, and God saw that they were very good.

On the sixth day, God said, "Let there be animals of every kind." And so there were, both wild and tame. And God blessed the animals, every one.

Now God was pleased, seeing that all of this work was very, very good. But there were no people yet, and so God made man and woman, giving them both a likeness to the Being and the Spirit of their Maker.

Then, on the seventh day, God rested.

ADAM AND EVE

THE FIRST MAN made by God was Adam, and the first woman was Eve. God planted a garden in Eden for them, and said to them, "You may have anything here that you want, only do not eat from this one tree, here in the garden. If you do, you will die."

Now there was a snake in the garden, and one day he said to Eve, "Did God really tell you not to eat this? Try a little taste; it won't hurt you." The fruit did look delicious. So Eve ate some and gave some to Adam, and he ate. Then Adam and Eve heard God walking in the garden in the cool of the day, and they tried to hide. "Why are you hiding from me?" God called to Adam. "What have you done? Have you eaten the one thing I told you not to eat?"

"It was Eve's fault," said Adam. "She gave it to me." "It was the snake's fault," said Eve. "He made me want to taste it."

Then God said to the snake, "You will be punished for this." And to Adam and Eve God said, "You have done the only thing I told you not to do. So you must go now, out into the world where you will have to work and struggle very hard, and you will have to die someday." But before they went away, God took animal skins and made clothes to comfort and protect them.

CAIN AND ABEL

AFTER THEY LEFT EDEN, Adam and Eve had two sons. The first was Cain, who was a farmer. The next was Abel, who kept sheep. One day Cain brought the best of his crops, and Abel brought the first-born of his lambs, as holy offerings to God. But God was pleased only with Abel's lamb.

Cain went away angry. And God came after him, saying, "Lift up your head, Cain! This behavior is not good for you." But Cain would not listen, because he was thinking only of himself. Soon he was so furious that he turned upon his brother in the fields one day, and killed him.

Then God came after him again, asking, "Where is your brother?" But Cain lied to God, and said, "I do not know. Am I my brother's keeper?"

And God said, "I know what you have done! The blood of Abel is crying out to me from the ground. This land will grow nothing good for you now. You must go away, Cain, and never come back again."

Noah's Ark

WHEN PEOPLE WENT on hurting one another, and spoiling the beautiful world that was so new, God sent a great flood that washed it clean again. But God remembered one good man, whose name was Noah, and spoke to him, saying, "Noah, you must build an ark, and into the ark put all of your family, and plenty of food. Then bring a pair of animals of every kind, and two of every creeping thing, and also of every bird alive." Noah did all this. And God closed the door of the ark for him—and then it began to rain.

And it rained and it rained and it rained, for forty days and forty nights. The waters rose until every other living creature was drowned, but the ark floated safely upon the flood. It landed at last upon Mount Ararat.

And when the waters had gone down, Noah and all his passengers came out of the ark and stood upon dry land, giving thanks to God for saving them. The sun was shining once again, and when they looked up they saw a beautiful rainbow in the sky. Then God said to Noah, "Whenever you see a rainbow, let it be a sign to you that I will never send such a flood again. And for your part, the people on earth must be kind to one another from now on, and they are now in charge of all my creatures."

THE TOWER OF BABEL

AFTER THE FLOOD the children of Noah had children, and soon there were many people on earth again. At this time they were all part of the same family, and they all spoke the same language.

Now the people of Babylon learned how to make bricks, and how to build with them. This made them very proud indeed. One day they said, "Let us build a great tower! Let us build it so high that it will reach all the way to heaven!" In this way, they wished to show all the world that they were as great and powerful as God.

But God saw them working on their tower and thought, "What will these children do next? I had better stop them before they are in serious trouble!"

And so on that day God made the people of earth speak different languages. Suddenly, the proud builders of Babylon could not understand one another. They never finished building their tower. Instead, they went away to live in foreign places. And even now, the people of different countries speak different languages.

ABRAHAM'S JOURNEY

IN A TOWN CALLED HARAN there lived a wise old man named Abraham with his wife Sarah. Abraham had many servants, and many herds of cattle, and much gold. Sarah was strong, and clever, and very beautiful. Still, they were sad because they had no children.

One day God came to Abraham and said, "I want you and Sarah to leave this home of yours. Bring your servants with you, and bring your cattle and your gold, for I will show you another place to live, in a different country. And there your family will become a great nation, one that will bring a blessing to the whole world."

Abraham was amazed, but without wasting time he did as God had told him. It was a long, long journey through deserts and over rivers, and all that time they did not know where they were going. At last they came to a pass between great mountains, and looked out at the rich green countryside of Canaan. "This land shall be yours forever," said God.

And as Abraham lay down to rest, God spoke to him again, saying, "Look up at the stars, Abraham. Count them, if you can. You have no sons or daughters now, but that is how many children will be born someday, into your family."

Isaac and Rebekah

GOD ALWAYS KEPT PROMISES. Even though Abraham and Sarah were very, very old by now they had a baby, and they named him Isaac, which means, "God has laughed with joy." Of all the gifts that God had given them, their little son Isaac was most dear.

As Isaac grew to be a man, Abraham thought, "We live among strangers here who do not know our ways." And he told his chief servant, "You must go back to our homeland and find a good woman there, to be my son's wife."

So the faithful servant made the long journey again; and at last he came, tired and thirsty one night, to the place of Nahor. The women were coming for water at the village well, and the servant watched them, praying, "God, help me to find the wife you want for Isaac. If she is here, let her show her kindness by bringing water to me, and also to my camels."

Just then he saw the most beautiful maiden of all, and her name was Rebekah. "Please, may I have some water?" the servant asked her. Rebekah was very kind; she gave him plenty of water to drink, and then she ran again to the well, saying, "Wait—for your camels must be thirsty too!"

That is how Rebekah came to be chosen as the wife of Isaac. And when they met, they loved each other at first sight.

JOSEPH AND HIS BROTHERS

ISAAC'S SON WAS JACOB, and he had a son called Joseph, who was a shepherd boy. Young Joseph had wonderful dreams, but his brothers did not like to hear of them. He had a fine coat, but they did not like to see it, for they were envious. At last one day they took Joseph out into the desert, meaning to get rid of him. But God was watching over him, and so instead Joseph was taken by a band of travelers to the land of Egypt, far away.

There he was a slave and a prisoner, but still the God of Israel kept him safe and also gave Joseph the power to understand dreams. One day Pharaoh said, "Bring me that prisoner! I think he can explain the strange dream I have had." Joseph listened, and then told him, "It means that hard times are coming. We must be ready." Pharaoh replied, "Then you shall be my chief steward, and store up food for all of us." Joseph did this so well that no one went hungry in the land of Egypt.

Yet, there was hunger in the land of Israel. And now, Joseph's brothers came to Egypt to buy food. When they were brought before the chief steward and saw that he was their long-lost brother Joseph, they were ashamed. But Joseph said, "I forgive you, for this has all been part of God's plan." And he embraced them, and gave them all the food they could carry home.

BABY MOSES

AFTER JOSEPH'S DAY there was a cruel new Pharaoh who made slaves of all the Israelites living in his country. And in time they were so angry about this that Pharaoh began to be afraid of them. "There are too many of these foreigners in Egypt now," he said. "We must do something about them, or else they may rise up against us!"

So, Pharaoh made a law that all baby boys born to the Israelites must be drowned in the river. But one brave Israelite mother kept her baby and hid him away from Pharaoh's soldiers. At last she could hide him no longer. She put the baby into a basket that was safe and dry, and placed the basket among the reeds at the edge of the river. And his sister Miriam watched over him, from a secret hiding place nearby.

Soon Pharaoh's daughter came with her maidens to bathe in the river. "Listen!" said the princess. "Someone is crying!" When the baby was found, she took him into her arms. "This is one Israelite child who shall not be harmed," she said, "for I will keep him as my own!" Miriam came forward now and asked, "Shall I find you a nurse?" "Yes!" said the princess. The girl ran quickly for their mother. And so it was that the real mother of Moses came to be his nurse, and cared for him until he was grown.

THE BURNING BUSH

MOSES GREW UP as a prince in Egypt, but he was not happy, seeing that his own people were kept there as slaves. One day, while tending sheep in the wilderness, Moses suddenly saw a great light before him. It seemed to come from a bush that was blazing and burning, without being destroyed.

"Moses, Moses!" called a voice from the flames. "Here am I," he replied. "I am the God of Israel," said the voice; "I am the God of Abraham, Isaac, and Jacob before you. I have seen my children's pain, and I have chosen you to bring them to freedom. Go to Pharaoh now, and tell him, *Let my people go!*"

"But Pharaoh will not listen to me!" answered Moses, hiding his face, for he was afraid to look at God.

"I shall make him listen," said God. "And Egypt shall be punished. Fear not, Moses; I will give you all the power you need. But for your part, you must remember this: teach your children and your children's children that I AM. Tell them always how I saw their suffering, and was moved to help them. For I will set my people free now, but they must remember forever that it was I who brought them out of slavery, and into the Promised Land."

CROSSING THE SEA

MANY PUNISHMENTS CAME down on Egypt; and just as God had promised, the People of Israel were finally allowed to leave. At first the cruel Pharaoh thought, "I am glad to be rid of them. They and that God of theirs are too much trouble!" But the next day he said to his soldiers, "Those Israelites were good workers. We need them! Come, let us follow them and make them come back!"

The Israelites had run away suddenly, taking only a few belongings, and their unleavened bread. Now they stood at the edge of a wide sea, and when they heard Pharaoh and all his mighty army coming after them, they were terrified. "This is your fault, Moses," they cried. "Why did you bring us out here to die?"

"Do not be afraid," Moses told them. "God is watching over us. God will bring us to the Promised Land." Then Moses raised his hand, and the waters parted. Quickly the Israelites ran across.

But when the army of Egypt tried to follow them, God sent the sea flooding back. And all of Pharaoh's soldiers were drowned, and all his great warhorses. And all their armor and their weapons were lost, and all their mighty chariots.

TEN COMMANDMENTS

THE PEOPLE OF ISRAEL had much to learn before they would be ready to enter the Promised Land. And so God made them wander in the wilderness for forty years. All that time God watched over them, and gave them food from heaven to eat, and taught them what they needed to know.

At last they came to a holy place called Mount Sinai, where they saw a cloud upon the mountaintop, and a fire within the cloud. Everyone was frightened. But Moses climbed the mountain all alone until he was face to face with God. And from the heart of the fire God spoke to him, saying:

1. Remember: only I am God.
2. Do not make or worship any idol.
3. Keep my name holy.
4. Rest and pray on the Sabbath.
5. Respect your parents.
6. Do no murder.
7. In marriage, be faithful.
8. Do not steal.
9. Do not lie.
10. Do not be greedy or envious.

Moses carved these Ten Commandments in stone so that no one would ever forget them. And the people made an ark, so that they could carry the stones with them wherever they went.

THE WALLS OF JERICHO

WHEN MOSES WAS very old he told the People of Israel, "After I die, Joshua will be your leader. Follow him! He is wise and brave. Soon you will be coming into the place of milk and honey which is the Promised Land. And you will have to fight for it, but do not be afraid!

"Remember to love our God with all your mind and all your heart and all your strength. Be faithful to the God of Israel and keep the Commandments! Then God will always help you, for this is promised—this is our Covenant."

When Moses died, he was buried in a secret place known only to God. And then the day came when Joshua led the Israelites across the River Jordan, for their first great battle at the city of Jericho. Around and around the high walls of the city marched the fighting men of Israel, once each day for six days in a row. And seven priests marched with them carrying the Ark of the Covenant, and sounding seven trumpets made of rams' horns. On the seventh day they all marched seven times around the walls of the city. Then the priests blew loud and long upon their trumpets, and all the Israelites gave a mighty shout. And then—the walls of Jericho came tumbling down!

The Story of Ruth and Naomi

ONCE THERE WAS A WOMAN from Bethlehem named Naomi, who went to live in the land of Moab far away. There her son married a girl called Ruth, and Ruth became Naomi's daughter-in-law, and also her dearest friend. But in time, Naomi's husband died, and her son died also. Naomi was all alone now, in a foreign land. One day she said to Ruth, "I do not want to leave you, but I must go home now to my own people, and you will do well to stay here with your mother."

"Do not ask me ever to leave you," Ruth told her. "For wherever you go, there will I go also. And wherever you live, that shall be my home. Your people shall be my people from now on, and your God shall be my God."

So it was that the two women made their way together back to Bethlehem. And Ruth took good care of her mother-in-law, and worked hard in the fields to gather food for both of them. But the owner of the fields noticed Ruth, and loved her, seeing that she was brave and kind and good. Soon they were married. When their first child was born, old Naomi was filled with joy. Now she had a family to care for once again! And long, long after this, Ruth became the grandmother, and Naomi the great-grandmother, of David, King of Israel.

Tony Chen

LITTLE SAMUEL

THERE WAS ONCE in the land of Israel a woman named Hannah who wanted more than anything to have a child. She prayed to God, saying, "Please, if you will send me a son, then I promise that he will serve you forever!" And God heard her prayer.

Soon a baby boy was born to her, and Hannah sang for joy. When little Samuel was old enough, she took him to the temple. There he worked and studied under the chief priest, a man named Eli, and his mother came there to visit him.

One night the boy heard a voice in the temple saying, "Samuel! Samuel!" At first he thought that Eli must be calling him. "No," said Eli, "I did not call." And this happened three times over, until Eli understood at last that little Samuel was hearing the voice of God. "If God calls again," said Eli, "you must say, 'Speak, Almighty, your servant is listening.' "

"Speak, Almighty, your servant is listening," said Samuel when he heard the voice once more. And then God spoke to him, telling him what must be done to save Israel. From this time on, Samuel became a great prophet and a great leader—one who listened carefully to God, and did what God wanted him to do.

Tony Chen

THE SHEPHERD BOY

WHEN SAMUEL THE PROPHET was a very old man the Israelites said, "We want to be like other people, and that means we must have a king." Samuel asked God what to do. "Give them a king," said God. And so Samuel chose a big, good-looking fighting man named Saul. And Saul tried to be a good king, but he did so many things wrong that Samuel was sorely disappointed. At last God said to Samuel, "Do not worry about Saul any more. I have already chosen a new king for Israel, from Jesse's family."

So Samuel went to look for the new king at the home of Ruth's grandson, Jesse. There he found seven fine young men who were Jesse's sons, and the eldest was very tall and good-looking. "This must be the new king," thought Samuel, but then God spoke to him, saying, "No, Samuel, you are wrong. Men and women see only how a person looks on the outside. God judges by what is in the heart."

"Have you another child?" Samuel asked Jesse. "Yes," Jesse said, "but he is only a boy, out tending the sheep." "Send for him," said Samuel, and Jesse did. When David came in—a simple shepherd boy with shining eyes—Samuel looked at him, and listened quietly for God's word. After a moment he said, "Yes, this is the one!"

David and Goliath

WHEN DAVID WAS YOUNG, the People of Israel were fighting the Philistines. A giant called Goliath stood up from the Philistine army one day and said, "I will fight any man who dares to come against me." But no one dared, because he was so strong that they all were terrified.

As David was bringing food to his brothers on the battlefield, he heard all this and said, "I will try to fight Goliath, and God will help me." But his brothers scorned him, and the giant laughed and said, "Come, little one, and try it, for I will feed your flesh to the birds!"

King Saul said, "You are much too young for this, David. But if you must fight him, at least take my armor and my sword." David would not take them, however. He was only a shepherd boy, unused to such things. Instead, he took his sling and five smooth stones from the river. While the giant was still laughing at him, he quickly ran forward, sending a stone straight at Goliath's head.

The stone hit Goliath and he fell face down on the ground in all his heavy armor. Then David took the giant's own sword and cut off his head. At this, the Israelites sent up a great cheer for David, and all the Philistines ran away.

DAVID AND SOLOMON

WHEN DAVID GREW UP he was a great man—a singer of songs, a maker of poems, and a bold warrior-king of Israel. It was David who danced in the streets as he brought the Ark of the Covenant into Jerusalem. And he wanted to build a temple there for it, but God said, No.

"You are a fighting man, David," God told him. "I want a man of peace to build my house." And so it was David's son Solomon who later built a splendid temple in Jerusalem, and put the Ark inside it. And Solomon listened carefully to God, and prayed that he might be a good king.

Now came a time of joy and riches for Israel. The ships and camels of Solomon the King went to the ends of the earth to bring back precious stones and gold, spices and fruits, and all things rare and beautiful.

Far away in Arabia, the Queen of Sheba heard of Israel's glory. She was surprised that these rough fighting men had built such a kingdom, and one day she came to see it for herself. King Solomon gave a great feast for her, with delicacies served on golden platters. Afterward, the two talked alone together long into the night. And when the wise king had answered her every question, the Queen of Sheba said, "Blessed are you! And great indeed is the God of Israel!"

AHAB AND ELIJAH

AFTER SOLOMON, the Israelites had some good kings and some bad ones; but the worst of all was Ahab of Jezreel. King Ahab and Queen Jezebel did not love God. Instead, they worshipped an idol named Baal, and for the sake of this false god, they did many evil things.

At that time the Prophet of God was Elijah, a man of great authority. Elijah went to Ahab and said, "Stop this, or you will have no more rain. God has said so, and Baal cannot help you!" From that day on, the hot sun shone down always. The wicked king was furious, but what could he do? Elijah was hiding in a cave where no one could find him, and all the crops went dry and died, and all the people were starving.

Finally Ahab and Jezebel gave up. It was true: Baal could not help them. And now Elijah, coming out of his cave, made a great offering on the mountaintop. When God came down to light the flames of that holy fire for Elijah, all the people cried, "The God of Israel is the only God!"

"Mend your wicked ways!" Elijah told King Ahab. Then he said, "You might as well go home now. Listen! Here comes the rain." The king rode away in his splendid chariot. But the hand of God was upon Elijah, so that he tucked up his cloak and ran ahead of Ahab, all the way to Jezreel.

JONAH

ONCE THERE WAS A PROPHET named Jonah who tried to run away from God. He did not want to do what God told him, so he took a ship and sailed as far away as he could go.

After a time a bad storm came up, and everyone on the ship was frightened. Jonah was the only one not praying. "Maybe this is your fault, Jonah," the sailors said. "It seems that God of yours is angry now!" And they were sorry about it, but to save the ship they threw him overboard.

God *was* angry, and yet, did not let Jonah drown. Instead, God sent a huge fish to swallow him. For three days Jonah was down in the dark inside the fish. All that time he was praying to God to come and save him. And all that time, of course, God was watching over Jonah inside the big fish, down under the water far away. And God was hearing Jonah's prayers.

After three days God made the fish vomit Jonah up, so that he landed safely on the shore. Now that he was safe, Jonah wondered what to do next. "Now that you are safe," God said to him, "are you going to do what I told you in the first place?"

"Yes," said Jonah. And he did.

AND A LITTLE CHILD

"HOLY, HOLY, HOLY, great God of Hosts, Heaven and Earth are full of your glory!" This was the hymn sung by angels in the great Temple at Jerusalem; and a young man named Isaiah heard it. Long after King David and King Solomon, these were times of trouble for the

people of Israel. They had forgotten God's Covenant, and no longer obeyed the Commandments.

Isaiah became a great prophet. "Stop being greedy and cruel!" he said. "Remember that you are God's people! You are supposed to do what is right and good." Then he promised the Israelites that a child filled with God's spirit would be born into David's family, and that he would be called a Prince of Peace. "When he comes," said Isaiah, "the people who have walked in darkness shall see a great light. And the wolf shall walk with the lamb, and the calf with the lion; and a little child shall lead them. And there shall be no hurt, no harm, in all my holy mountain."

Songs About God

PRAISE GOD! SAY THE beautiful songs called Psalms. Let everything that lives sing praises to our Maker! For God our Creator is all-powerful. Yet, at God's altar, the littlest sparrow has a nesting place.

Let us give thanks with our whole hearts for all of God's world—for the stars, and for wind; for the moon shining bright in the dark night sky. And let us thank God for sunshine also, and for rain, and rainbows—for all the earth that we love so much, with its mountains and its meadows, its gentle rivers and its great, thundering seas.

And let us give thanks for God's Commandments, that teach us how to be good. Happy are those who do what is right, and say what is true. Happy are those who obey God's laws and remember God's promises always.

And let us give thanks above all for God's love, in which each of us is safe as a child at its mother's breast. God fills the hungry with good things. We are the apple of God's eye. We are sheltered under the shadow of God's great wings. Happy are those who trust like little children in their Maker, for out of the mouths of the smallest babies come God's praises! Surely, goodness and mercy will follow them all the days of their lives.

THE STORY OF THE MACCABEES

THERE CAME A TIME when enemies of Israel had taken Jerusalem, and they tried to make the people bow down to their Greek god, Zeus.

A Jewish boy of Israel, named Judas Maccabeus, was growing up with his four brothers in the small town named Modin. And when the pagan Greeks came there with soldiers, trying to make everyone worship their false gods, the boys' father stepped forth boldly, saying that he would not do it. Then he and his sons fled into the mountains, leaving all they owned behind them. They gathered a band of brave warriors, and in time Judas Maccabeus became their leader.

For three years they fought against Greek armies until at last they recaptured Jerusalem. How terrible it was to find their beloved Temple all spoiled and ruined by the enemy! But the Maccabees and their comrades worked hard to make it clean; and when that was done, they worshipped God in the Temple once again. And they burned sweet-smelling incense, and lit the lamps of the Temple one by one. Then, while the lamps burned for eight days, all Israel gave thanks to God, and celebrated, and rejoiced.

This was the first Feast of Lights. And it is still remembered every year, during the happy, holy time called Hanukkah.

THE
·NEW TESTAMENT·

CHILD OF GOD

IN THE BEGINNING God said, "Let there be light!" and there was light. And yet, the world was often a dark and troubled place.

Then, after a long time, something wonderful happened. A child was born who was like the light that helps us see our way in darkness. And this was because the child belonged to God, and because he had been a part of God from the beginning.

People had been waiting and waiting for him. At last one day an angel came to a young girl called Mary in the town of Nazareth. And the angel greeted her saying, "Hail, O blessed one!" Mary was troubled at first, but the angel said, "God is with you, Mary. Do not be afraid.

"Soon you will have a baby that comes from God," the angel told her. "His name will be Jesus. He will be a great king someday, and he will rule the world forever."

"How can this happen?" asked Mary. "I know no man to be the father of this child."

"For the Creator, all things are possible," the angel answered. Then Mary said, "I am glad to serve my God. Let it be as you have said."

JESUS IS BORN

ONE STARRY NIGHT in the little town of Bethlehem, Mary's baby was born. And she brought him into the world in a stable, because they were far from home, and there was no room at the inn.

And the angel of God came to shepherds who watched their flocks in the fields by night, saying, "Fear not! I bring you news of great joy to all people.

The holy child is born who is your Savior, Christ the Lord! Let this be a sign to you: you will find him in Bethlehem, wrapped in swaddling cloths, lying in a manger." Then, suddenly, the whole sky was filled with angels, singing "Glory to God in the highest; peace on earth!"

Quickly the shepherds came and found the newborn King with his mother Mary, and Joseph her husband, and the farm animals all around them, quiet and wondering. And the shepherds saw that Jesus was the Holy Child of God, and they knelt down and worshipped him.

FLIGHT INTO EGYPT

WHEN JESUS WAS BORN, a great star was seen shining in the East. Three wise men marveled at the sight, and set out to follow the star, hoping to learn its meaning. When they had come as far as Jerusalem they said to King Herod, who ruled under the Romans there, "This is a mighty sign! Has a powerful new prince been born in recent days?" The king was angry and alarmed. "Let me know what you discover," he told them. Herod had a plan.

The wise men rode on to Bethlehem, and there found that the star stood still over the stable where Jesus lay. They were amazed that any prince should be in such a place. But when they saw the child, they knelt down on the straw in all their splendid robes. And they gave to him the richest gifts they had to offer: gold, and frankincense, and myrrh.

Now when the wise men left Bethlehem, they went home by another way, for they did not want Herod to find Jesus and try to do him harm. The wicked king was furious when he learned this. "Kill every baby you can find!" he told his soldiers. They spread terror throughout the country, but the angel of God warned Joseph in a dream. He awakened Mary, and they carried Jesus quickly out into the night, and fled to the land of Egypt, far away.

WHEN JESUS WAS A BOY

AFTER HEROD WAS DEAD it was safe for Mary and Joseph to bring young Jesus home again. He grew up with them in the little town of Nazareth, in Galilee; and Mary wondered about all the strange things that had happened, and turned them over in her mind.

Each year the family traveled to Jerusalem to worship in the Temple at Passover time, when all the Jews of Israel tried to gather in their great House of God, remembering how they had been brought out of Egypt.

Jesus was always with them. But during their visit when the boy was twelve years old, Mary and Joseph suddenly missed him on the way home to Nazareth, and could not find him anywhere. Back to Jerusalem they hurried, anxious and fearful, searching high and low.

At last they thought to look for him in the Temple, and there was Jesus, calmly sitting in the midst of all the rabbis and the elders. And he was asking them questions, and also answering their questions with such intelligence that everyone was amazed. Mary could hardly believe her own eyes. "We have been so worried!" she cried to her son. "How could you do such a thing to us?" But Jesus calmly replied, "Did you not know that I must be in my Father's House?"

JOHN THE BAPTIST

WHEN JESUS WAS A YOUNG MAN there was a famous prophet living in the wilderness, one who wore a shirt made of camel's hair, and ate locusts and wild honey. People came from far away to hear him speak, and he told them that they were all sinners, needing to be saved. If they were sorry, he baptized them in the River Jordan as a sign that their sins were washed away. And for this reason, he was called John the Baptist.

People asked John, "Are you the Savior we have been waiting for?" But he always answered, "No. Someone else is coming, far, far greater than I."

Then one day Jesus came to the river. John looked into his eyes, and then he said, "Lord, it is you who ought to baptize me." But Jesus replied, "Even so, this should be done." And so the two went to the river, and Jesus was baptized. At that moment, they saw the Spirit of God like a dove descending, and they heard the voice of God saying, "This is my beloved Son, in whom I am well pleased!"

Afterward John told his people, "This is the Savior we have waited for! He is the Lamb of God, who takes away the sins of the world. I have baptized you with water, but Jesus Christ will baptize you with the Holy Spirit of God."

THE WEDDING

SOME OF JOHN THE BAPTIST'S PEOPLE began to follow Jesus everywhere, and they were also his disciples. One day they were invited, with Jesus and his mother Mary, to a wedding in the village of Cana. The bridegroom's house was filled with friends and relations singing, dancing, and feasting. After a time, they ran out of wine.

"They have no more wine!" Mary whispered to Jesus. But he turned away from her, saying, "My hour has not come yet." Even so, Mary said to the servants, "do whatever my son tells you!"

Now, six stone jars were standing nearby, which were used for water to purify the hands before mealtime. Each jar held twenty or thirty gallons. "Fill these jars with water," Jesus said. And the servants came and filled them to the brim. "Now take some out, and take it to the feast." Again they did as he said. When the toastmaster tried it, the water had turned to wine, and he went to the bridegroom in amazement. "This is the best wine of all," he cried, "yet you have saved it for the last!"

The wedding guests did not know what had happened, but the disciples saw it all. They believed in Jesus. And this was his first miracle, which was done at Cana in Galilee.

THE FISHERMEN

NOW JESUS BEGAN TO WALK from place to place in Galilee, speaking to the people, and healing them. "The Spirit of God is upon me," he told them. "God has sent me to bring good news to the poor, to comfort the brokenhearted. I have come bringing freedom to all slaves and prisoners. I have come to heal the blind, that they may see."

One day, while Jesus was walking by the edge of the Sea of Galilee, he noticed two fishermen casting their nets into the water. Andrew and Simon were brothers, who worked hard at their trade. Jesus stopped to watch them for a time. Then he said to them, "Follow me, for I will make you fishers of human beings!" There and then, Simon and Andrew left their nets and followed Jesus. And he gave Simon another name: *Peter,* which means "Rock."

A little farther on that day, Jesus saw two more fishermen sitting in a boat, mending nets. He called to them: "Follow me!" So James the son of Zebedee, and John his brother also came to Jesus, and followed him. And everywhere Jesus went, he told the people, "God has sent me to bring a new way of life to you. I have come to teach you about the kingdom of heaven, for it is closer than you think."

SERMON ON THE MOUNT

FINDING A GREAT CROWD around him one day, Jesus went to the top of a small hill so that people could see and hear him better. There he spoke of the coming of God's kingdom. "The new way of life does not mean that you may forget the Law and the Commandments," he said. "You must always honor those, and act upon them. But I tell you that good actions are not enough. You must also take great care of your secret thoughts, for God wants your hearts to be true, and filled with goodness." Then he said:

Blessed are you who want God's love, and feel that you do not deserve it; you belong in the Kingdom.

Blessed are you who are gentle; God will give the whole earth to you.

Blessed are you whose hearts are full of pain; God will give you strength and comfort.

Blessed are you who hunger and thirst after justice; you will be satisfied.

Blessed are you who forgive those who have wronged you; God will forgive you also.

Blessed are you who love God with singleness of heart; you shall see your Creator face to face.

Blessed are you who make peace; you are God's very own.

THE LORD'S PRAYER

THEN JESUS SAID, "You know that it is good to share what you have, and to help the needy. It is even better to do such things quietly, without asking for attention. God knows what you are doing and will reward you. And even before you begin to say your prayers, God knows what you want to ask, and what your needs are. So do not make a great show of yourself, praying. Instead, go into a quiet place by yourself and say something simple, like this:

Our Father in heaven,

Hallowed be your name.

Your kingdom come,

Your will be done,

On earth as in heaven.

Give us today our daily bread,

And forgive us our sins

As we forgive those who sin against us.

Save us from the time of trial

And deliver us from evil. Amen.

PLANTING SEEDS

"THE KINGDOM OF HEAVEN is like a mustard seed," said Jesus. "This is the littlest seed of all, but it grows and grows, into a huge plant. And then it still keeps growing until it is a tremendous tree, so high that the birds of the air come and build their nests in it."

When Jesus told this parable he was in a boat, because so many people had come to the water's edge to hear him speak. Some of them did not understand this story, and so he told another:

"A farmer went out one day to plant seeds. Some fell onto a pathway, where birds ate them. Others fell upon rocks, where their roots could not grow strong, and so they withered. Some fell among thorny weeds, and they died. But the last of the seeds fell into good, rich earth, and they brought a splendid harvest for the farmer."

"Master, please explain the story!" said the disciples. And Jesus said, "God is the farmer. The seeds are the truths God wants me to share with you in these stories. The good, rich earth is the heart of a person who loves me and makes space for my words to grow in. If yours is such a heart, my stories will unfold their meaning within you. And God will rejoice to see your life becoming strong, and useful, and beautiful."

Jesus and the Children

WHEN JESUS WAS TRAVELING from place to place in the countryside, many people came to him, carrying their babies and holding their small children by the hand. "Please give your blessing to our young ones," they asked. But the followers of Jesus tried to send them away. Jesus saw this happening, and he said, "Let the little children come to me!"

Then he took the smallest one up in his arms, and showed her to the grown people. "If you are not glad to see little ones like this, you will not get into my kingdom," Jesus said.

"Oh please," cried the child's mother. "Let me take her! Do not let her bother you! I only wanted your blessing, so that she might grow up to be an important person someday."

"Children are important already," Jesus told her. "No one in all the world is greater than the smallest of these. No one is closer to God, for guardian angels are watching over them always. And remember this: anyone who is cruel to a little child would be better off at the bottom of the sea. But the person who loves a child, and tells her the truth, and helps her to be good, is loved by God forever. Never forget: when you help a little child, you are helping me."

MARTHA AND MARY

IN THE VILLAGE OF BETHANY near Jerusalem there lived two sisters; one was called Martha, and the other was called Mary. When he was nearby, Jesus often stopped to visit them.

Both Martha and Mary loved Jesus, and they were overjoyed to see him. But when he came into their house, Martha found little time to spend with her guest, for she was always rushing about, fixing special foods for him and making a great ado about the serving. Mary did not do any of this. Instead, she sat quietly listening to Jesus, and thinking long and deep about every word that he said.

One day Martha worked so hard and fussed so much over all her arrangements that she put herself into a bad temper. She came to Jesus and said, "Master, I am doing all of this work alone, and look—my sister is not doing anything! Why don't you make her come and help me?"

Now, Jesus loved both Mary and Martha. He also understood that the two sisters were very different. "Martha, Martha!" he said. "You busy yourself with so many things, but most of them are not needed. Mary is doing something more important, now. She is paying attention to me, and you must not take that away from her!"

A Man Is Healed

WHEN JESUS WAS in the town of Capernaum, so many people came to him wanting to hear his words, and hoping to be healed, that they could not all fit into the little house where he was staying. Then a man came who was ill, lying on a mat with four friends carrying him, because he was paralyzed and could not walk.

But they could not make their way through the crowd, and so the four men climbed onto the roof of the house and made an opening there. Then they took some ropes and lowered their sick friend down into the room where Jesus sat. And Jesus was pleased, seeing how great their faith was. "My son, your sins are forgiven," he said to the paralyzed man. "Take up your mat and walk!" And the man rose up right away and walked home, much to everyone's amazement.

But Jesus had many enemies by now, who wanted to hurt him. Some of them were watching all of this, and they grew furious. They were thinking secretly, "How dare he say that he forgives sins! Only God has that authority!" Jesus knew what they were thinking. "Why do you doubt me?" he asked. "You heard my words. You saw what happened. The man is healed! And yes, I do have that authority."

LOAVES AND FISHES

JESUS AND HIS DISCIPLES crossed a lake by boat one day, hoping to find a quiet place to rest. However, many people ran around the lake and waited for them on the other side. So Jesus began again to teach them, and when evening came, they were all still there.

Seeing that they were hungry, Jesus told his disciples to feed them. "We do not have enough money to buy food for such a crowd," the disciples said. "Go and see how many loaves of bread you have," Jesus replied. The disciples counted, and said, "There are only five loaves and two fishes."

So Jesus told everyone to sit down in groups on the grass. And he blessed the food and broke it, and the disciples gave it to the people. They ate and ate, but there was always more, until everyone was completely satisfied. After that, twelve baskets were filled with all that was left.

When the people saw the wonders Jesus worked, they began to shout, "He is our Savior! He is the leader who will help us destroy our enemies!" And they tried to seize him and crown him king by force. But the Son of God was not that kind of Savior. His kingdom was not of worldly power, but of the heart and soul. And so he slipped away from them all and climbed alone far up into the hills, to pray.

THE LAST SUPPER

WHEN JESUS WENT TO JERUSALEM for the last time, he knew that his enemies were going to kill him. And so he gathered his disciples in a hidden upper room to share the Passover Seder with them once more. Taking bread, he gave thanks and broke it, and gave it to his disciples, saying, "Take, eat. This is my body which is broken for you. Do

this, always, in remembrance of me." Then, taking a cup of wine, he said, "Drink this, all of you, for it is my blood, which is poured out that the sins of the world may be forgiven. When I am gone, do this and remember me."

"Lord, please do not leave us," cried his disciples. Jesus replied, "I came from God, and now I must go back home. But I leave my peace with you—peace which is not of this world. Now you must love one another as I have loved you. And I will send my Holy Spirit, which is the Spirit of Truth, to help and comfort all who love me, forever."

DEATH AND RESURRECTION

AFTER THIS, soldiers took Jesus away, and beat him. Then he was crucified. When he was on the cross, Jesus said, "Father, forgive them, for they know not what they do." He died at three in the afternoon.

His weeping mother Mary wrapped the body of her son in linen cloth for burial, and it was placed in a nearby cave, with a heavy stone rolled against the entrance. Early in the morning, three women who had believed in Jesus and loved him came to the cave to bathe the body with precious oils. But the stone was rolled away, and the body was gone. Mary Magdalene began to cry. Then she heard a voice saying, "Why do you weep?" And there was Jesus, beside her. Death could not hold him. Jesus was risen!

Later that day the disciples were still grieving behind locked doors when suddenly they found Jesus among them. "Peace be with you!" he said. And then, seeing that they were afraid, "Look at me, touch me! I am flesh, not a ghost." And he sat with them, and took some broiled fish and ate it. Many, many others saw Jesus risen from the dead, and spoke with him, and some broke bread with him again, before his body was taken to heaven. So the disciples quickly took heart, and began teaching others the life and sayings of their gentle Master, Christ the Lord.

Saint Paul Tells the Good News

THERE WAS A MAN named Saul who hated Jesus, although he did not know him. Then, one day on the road to Damascus, Jesus came to him in a great white light, saying, "Saul, Saul, why do you try to hurt me?" Saul changed his mind, and changed his life, that day. His name became Paul, and he traveled the world telling people about Jesus. "This man was the Son of God," said Paul. "He came to show us God's love, to heal us and to teach us. He died to save us. Everyone on earth needs to know his story."

Sometimes Paul was ill, or hurt, or lost in storms at sea. Often he was in prison, for many people did not like what he told them. But Paul never gave up. Even in prison, he wrote great letters about Jesus, saying: He has sent his Holy Spirit to be with us always. Now we must work together, trying to be the Body of Christ on earth. Some of us are like hands, for giving and sharing. Some are like arms, reaching out to others and lifting them up, as Jesus would do. Others are like eyes and ears, showing people what is true, and helping them to act on it.

Three things are important, said Paul. They are faith, hope, and love—but the greatest of these is love. Our hearts are for loving one another, and all of God's world. Most of all they are for loving God, who is three in one: Creator, Christ, and Holy Spirit. Amen.

SANDOL STODDARD is well known to readers of all ages as the author of fourteen books for young people (including the prize-winning *Saint George and the Dragon*, *Five Who Found the Kingdom*, *Growing Time*, and the perennial best seller *I Like You*) and as a leading writer and lecturer on the hospice concept whose book on this subject, *The Hospice Movement: A Better Way of Caring for the Dying*, is regarded as definitive. For service to the hospice cause, she received special recognition from St. Christopher's Hospice, London, and the Humanitarian Award of the Forbes Health System in the United States. She has edited the journal, *Spiritual Journeys*, and has served on the boards of several interfaith organizations.

A magna cum laude graduate of Bryn Mawr and the mother of four grown sons, she now lives and writes in Kona, Hawaii.

TONY CHEN was one of America's foremost watercolorists, with a long list of honors, publications, and one-man shows. His paintings are in many museums and private collections throughout the country and have won awards from the Society of Illustrators, The American Institute of Graphic Arts, and the Children's Book Showcase. He has written and illustrated two books for children and illustrated over forty more.

Born in Jamaica, West Indies, he came to the United States in 1949 and received a B.F.A. with honors from Pratt Institute, Brooklyn. Most of his time was spent living and working Corona, New York.